WINNER OR LOSER:

Everything you need to know to invest in International Stock Exchange

...and something else

(English Version)

INCLUDED REAL CASE STUDIES

By

RUFINO VILLÉN FERNÁNDEZ

SUMMARY:

1. ABOUT THE AUTHOR

Rufino Villén Fernández, was born in Spain in 1976. He has a Diploma in Business Studies (2000), Bachelor of Business Administration (2002) from the Polytechnic University of Cartagena (UPCT) and Masters and Postgraduate Diploma in Applied Psychology and Ergonomics.

Likewise during his academic years at the Polytechnic University of Cartagena, he participated as a collaborator (1996-1997) and boarder (1997-1998) for the Department of Quantitative Methods for Economics at the University of Murcia.

On the other hand, at the same time during his university stage, he was employed from 1998 until 2002 in the banking sector with some of the most important banks worldwide.

His labor life has surprising twists, extending the versatility in diverse disciplines from the banking and financial sector until his step and professional development being employed for the Ministry of Defence in the Spanish Air Force.

Also, he has been working in the world of teaching, as teacher of mathematics, statistics and economics, as well as training programs teaching "Techniques for finding employment."

In addition, he has taken advantage of any opportunity where he could be actively involved in the participation in events and volunteer projects, developing and sharing activities with children with difficulties, disabilities, homeless or hospices, as well as in other activities of social interest.

He has been traveling by different international countries for years, knowing much of Europe, Latin America and Russia, always striving and eagerness to learn and to know directly and in first person, culture and original customs.

On November 17, 1999, he made his first investment in the Spanish Stock Exchange. He will not be forgotten. It was with the famous shares "Terra", and yes, the result was very satisfactory.

Surely at that time, he had no knowledge and skills on investment he has now. It is true that the practice and the experience during these years have led him to develop new techniques and investment methods.

Many years have passed from his first investment up to today, and it has been evolved greatly in technological systems, and certainly, there are much more information and tools to everyone regarding the information and tools that might exist in the years of his inception on Stock Exchange.

It is for that, since 1999, he is dedicated to research and constant study of diverse disciplines, among which are those aimed at the world of the Stock Exchange and economic-financial markets, that is to say, what is commonly called the Stock Exchange or Stock Market, as well as other types of financial products of similar typology as deposits, CFD, Forex, pension plans or retirement plans, investment funds, mortgages and so on.

His great adaptive and multidisciplinary capacity, they have got him great prestige and recognition in economic and financial aspect among their friends, colleagues and those people with whom he has directly participated and they have known him throughout these years, and which he has always been willing to help at all times.

2. ABOUT THE BOOK

One of the reasons by which this book has been elaborated is, among others, to demonstrate that if YOU really are interested for investing or to make profitable your savings in the "Stock Exchange", you could get it through the use of a basic "system" as well as some small guidelines.

In this book the utilization of a simple "system" as a tool of investment capable of being in use in what can be named "traditional Stock Exchange" on domestic and international markets, which in turn, this "system" could be implemented to make one comparative among other products that are directly related to the Stock Exchange and that "brokers" or "intermediaries" (banks, insurance agencies and so on.) offer you, and sometimes, these products offered by "brokers" are questioned because we do not have the knowledge adapted to be able to value them.

On the other hand, despite the availability on the market of thousands of books about the Stock Exchange, at all levels, and in which a huge amount of methods, systems, strategies and other skills are explained to become rich, millionaires or other analogies, this book is not to assess whether you are going to become rich investing in the Stock Exchange, then, because as you know in real life, it just will depend on YOU.

This book will empower you may be able to assimilate a new concept of understanding the "world of the Stock Exchange" or "investment world" simply and easily, without high academic knowledge or financial terms.

It may be the case that in other books on Stock Exchange, you had had certain difficulties in reading and comprehension, and therefore you were to waste the opportunity to take them to the practice. Therefore, with this book, some common problems that might arise in other books as they would be solved:

- In general, the most interesting books to start learning about the "World of the Stock Exchange", are technical books and are focused for professionals of the sector.

- Normally the "platforms" (applications or programs) to invest in the Stock Exchange, they offer a great quantity of information, tools and data that surely the great majority of those who are beginning in the "world of the Stock Exchange" are not capable of understanding completely the terms used because most of terminology used in these platforms are based on mathematics or statistics. If we add, that platforms may not be available in our country. The result you can achieve, it could be a real chaos.

-   On the other hand, companies or instructional cases where investments are focused on other books are companies in the domestic country, forgetting international companies from other countries.

In order to solve some of these common problems and that can appear in other books, it has been considered to edit and to publish at the same time this book in three different versions.

This book is available in a English version "**WINNER OR LOSER:** Everything you need to know to invest in International Stock Exchange... and something else", a Spanish version "**GANADOR O PERDEDOR:** Todas las cosas que debes saber para invertir en todos los Mercados Internacionales Bursátiles... y algo más" and a Russian version "**ПОБЕДИТЕЛЬ ИЛИ НЕУДАЧНИК:** все, что Вам нужно знать о том, как инвестировать в Международные Фондовые Биржи... и еще кое-что".

The great particularity that present these three books, is that in each version has been included some examples about REAL CASES with different companies.

Consequently and in certain way, the other two books "**GANADOR O PERDEDOR:** Todas las cosas que debes saber para invertir en todos los Mercados Internacionales Bursátiles... y algo más" and

"**ПОБЕДИТЕЛЬ ИЛИ НЕУДАЧНИК:** все, что Вам нужно знать о том, как инвестировать в Международные Фондовые Биржи… и еще кое-что" can be considered complementary to this one.

The reader has the option to verify that indeed the "system" used in this book can also be applied to other companies on International Stock Exchange, despite not having knowledge about Spanish or Russian language.

In these three books, they are going to use the same "system" in examples about real companies and, as we shall see, depending on how the "system" is implemented, it could be a great tool to invest in International Stock Exchange, regardless of the company or country in which you could be interested in investing. Also indicate that the examples about REAL CASES included in these three books, data processing are of March 2015.

If you have been interested also for reading other two books that have been mentioned previously, "**GANADOR O PERDEDOR:** Todas las cosas que debes saber para invertir en todos los Mercados Internacionales Bursátiles… y algo más" and "**ПОБЕДИТЕЛЬ ИЛИ НЕУДАЧНИК:** все, что Вам нужно знать о том, как инвестировать в Международные Фондовые Биржи… и еще кое-что", you will observe that, using the same "system" and adapting it to the target company, you can obtain optimal results.

Furthermore, to reduce the problem that sometimes can be found with the amount of information and tools provided on platforms Stock Exchange offered to the public, it has been chosen to work and apply in this book, one of the simplest "systems" that all platforms o Stock Exchange must have.

Also in these three books have been used as little as possible technicalities. It is the aim that the book will be useful for YOU from the beginning. Exactly, anyone can observe that in the examples about REAL CASES of the other two versions, "**GANADOR O PERDEDOR:** Todas las cosas que debes saber para invertir en todos los Mercados Internacionales Bursátiles... y algo más" and "**ПОБЕДИТЕЛЬ ИЛИ НЕУДАЧНИК:** все, что Вам нужно знать о том, как инвестировать в Международные Фондовые Биржи... и еще кое-что", without knowledge of the language, you could invest in those companies and countries, because the concepts and key ideas are written in an understandable and adequate teaching at all levels.

It is for what, it is considered that these three books are focused and are valid both for anyone who wants to delve into the world of the stock, since basic knowledge is transferred through a simple and clear language, as well as of several examples and case studies.

3. SOME WARNINGS AND RECOMMENDATIONS ABOUT THE BOOK AND INVESTMENT

Although the "system" exposed in this book is simple to use, nevertheless, it is necessary to consider some warnings and recommendations that investor must always keep in mind.

The "system" is presented in this book, is only a tool to help invest in "International Stock Exchange", but do not confuse it with the "Holy Grail".

Therefore, I indicated beforehand that the "system", as it is exposed and is demonstrated in this book, has worked for many years, but in addition to being a tool for investment, it is also a helpful tool to know if what the "brokers" offer us as an investment is worthwhile or not, that is to say, knowing what might be called the profit / risk ratio. Therefore, we must not forget and remember, it is always necessary to make a study of each investment in each particular case, either through our own, if we believe that we are able ourselves, or, if we are not sure, through "various" experts or professionals.

Before making any investment with your money -or money from another person-, make sure yourself that you have complete knowledge about the type of product where you are going to invest and also you understand perfectly the risk that you assume.

If this is your first contact with the Stock Exchange, I recommend you to keep learning a little more and do investment simulations -without real money-.

In addition how we all should know about this "world", past results do not guarantee future results.

Above all, I recommend you, never ask for credits or loans to invest in the Stock Exchange and never invest money you could need right away. In fact, before investing in "The Stock Exchange" or any other product, ask yourself **how much money you would be willing to lose?**

Remember responsible for your investment will be just YOU.

This book contains the opinions of the author and includes ideas, studies and strategies that may not be suitable for every individual. The Author and Publisher have strived to be as accurate and complete as possible in the creation of this book, notwithstanding the fact that they do not warrant or represent at any time that the contents within are accurate due to the rapidly changing nature of the Internet.

While all attempts have been made to verify information provided in this publication, the Author and Publisher assume no responsibility for errors, contrary interpretation of the subject matter herein.

You agree that the Author and Publisher are presenting this information as a guide and do not provide or confer to you any warranties, express or implied, for the products o services that are listed for your reference and will not be liable for our use of any product or service included in this book

All readers are advised to perform due diligence prior to purchase of any product or service mentioned herein. Any perceived slights of specific persons, peoples, or organizations are unintentional. In practical advice and guidebooks, like anything else in life, there are no guarantees on results. The Author and Publisher do not specifically endorse or guarantee the products and services listed herein, they are offering them as references for you to investigate further.

This book is a general guide and not intended for use as a source of legal, business, accounting, professional, or financial advice.

4. WHY ANOTHER BOOK OF STOCK EXCHANGE?

Thankfully, throughout many years, many people have allowed me to take part of them, to help and to teach friends, colleagues and acquaintances, both economic-financial aspects as personal, family, labor aspects and so on, but at the same time and the most curious thing is that, through each particular case with you or they, I have had the opportunity to obtain an apprenticeship or "feedback" which I have also learned a lot, perhaps more than many books could have taught me.

And perhaps for that reason, and in order to be grateful and to reward of somehow this "feedback" received and that each one of you have given, shared and taught me over the years by your personal experiences, mainly, that is why this book will be convey you, through a tool that is the Stock Exchange, how it would be possible return on investment of our savings, the ability to be financially independent, to enhance quality of life, to dedicate and to give more attention to family, friends, etc.

Therefore, in this book of Stock Exchange will capture some of the questions that most people at some point in their lives have raised interest in knowing and also offers the convenience of being able to convey a didactic, both people we already know each other, and to those others who I have not had the pleasure of meeting.

I think that YOU will be the protagonist and one of the main reasons for publishing this book, being also of great interest the fact that YOU could make extensible this knowledge to people who also care about.

In this book you will have the possibility of being able to improve investment of your savings, not only in the Stock Exchange but also for other financial products that may be attached to the Stock Exchange through the utilization of a simple "system" applied to the Stock Exchange.

Certainly, I cannot capture more than fifteen years of research and experience in a book, but you can pick up some of the most important points or strokes on the world of the stock happens.

If you are a beginner or this book is your first contact with the" world of the Stock Exchange", welcome to this "world" and, of course, congratulations for daring to learn a little more. Surely, this book is a good tool for your future investments, as well as to understand more about the workings of this great unknown "world" which you will find, as simple or complex as life itself.

The main goal is that YOU are who decides where to make your investments and know if you are really prepared to participate in this "world" or not. For this, a simple and clear vocabulary will be in use and I will use a simple "system" directly applied in examples about real companies in each book.

If you already have knowledge intermediate or advanced in the Stock Exchange, this book will remind you one of the more basic "systems", with which you surely would begin in this "world" and that sometimes with the passage of time and desire to excel in profits -or losses-, we forget because we are looking more complex "systems" and that these new systems cause more activity situations.

It is interesting that this book could be a useful tool to help people who often feel they do not have the sufficient knowledge to be able to decide on the investments of their savings.

Therefore, through actual cases described in detail, it will be observed directly that the "system" could be considered a good tool for investment, despite the years and new technologies developed. Likewise, you can also make sure that this "system" is extensible to companies and products internationally.

On the other hand in this book, in addition to focusing directly on share investments it is developing what might be called "financial education" with the intention to expand a little knowledge of real-world investment products that consistently offer us the "brokers" and that, generally, these products can be difficult to understand and therefore in many cases, we have to rely directly on what a "broker" or "employee" or "intermediary" tell us. At times, the "brokers" offer us different investment options and our ignorance, distrust or fear, we let escape certain opportunities and, conversely, we accept other investment options really are riskier and less profitable than the previous one.

In this book you will be offered the opportunity for a proper use of the "system", your savings could provide a complement for your future, which consequently could also be the future of your relatives, your children, and why not also so that together, we could help those who appreciate and have not had the opportunity to learn to invest the savings that much effort and sacrifice have cost them get during their lifetime.

5. ABOUT THE "SYSTEM"

The "system" used in this book, is the most basic and simple to learn in the "world of the Stock Exchange".

The "system" that is going to be applied in each and every the examples about real cases is thought to what we can call "traditional Stock Exchange", that is to say, we will be "Winners" when "Stock Exchange" go up, and will be "Losers" when "Stock Exchange" go down.

So, when the "system" is applied to examples about real cases presented in this book and in real cases also presented in the books **"GANADOR O PERDEDOR:** Todas las cosas que debes saber para invertir en todos los Mercados Internacionales Bursátiles... y algo más" and "**ПОБЕДИТЕЛЬ ИЛИ НЕУДАЧНИК:** все, что Вам нужно знать о том, как инвестировать в Международные Фондовые Биржи... и еще кое-что", in all these books, will be exhibited the specific dates on which the "system" indicates that it should have bought and the specific date on which the "system" indicates that it should have sold "shares", and where the benefits that could be obtained with its use are also detailed.

6. SOME OF THE PRINCIPLES TO BE WINNER OR LOSER

Those who know me in real life know that I do not like beating around the bush, and therefore I want to be straight from the beginning.

Therefore, especially for people interested in joining to the "world of the Stock Exchange", you should be remembered that in this "world", the first thing that is required to know is that YOU are the one who really "You Choose," that is to say, among the variety of companies or products on the market, you will have to choose which company or product you really want to invest. Furthermore, YOU are the one who "You Decide", that is to say, you have to decide willing to take the risk and amount of money to invest. Therefore, YOU are going to be responsible for "YOU Choice" and "YOU Decision".

Consequently, the decisions you have chosen you are going to get some results as Winner or Loser.

Therefore, previously to actively participate in this "world", we should consider, among others, certain principles of vital importance and could be considered interesting possess or develop, including:

- Self Confidence.
- Self-Discipline.
- Sacrifice.
- LOVE.

The "self-confidence" is essential in the "world of the Stock Exchange". The word "self-confidence", as its meaning implies, is to have confidence in you. It is impossible to invest in the "Stock Exchange if one is not sure what is going to do. In fact, if you are not sure of the investment to make, the best option, that you can choose in this case, is not investing.

It is true that the "system" that is developed in this book is quite simple, but if there is no confidence in you, it is best not to carry out the investment. You must know that in the world of "Stock Exchange", self-confidence is constantly testing for each investor demonstrates how confident he or she really possesses.

With the "self-discipline" the situation is similar as with the "self-confidence", that is to say, you must demonstrate a consistent discipline, following rules and keeping the marked from the beginning by yourself. As a person gets up every day to go to work and spend hours in his or her workplace keeping and obeying the rules established by the company, in the "world of the Stock Exchange" something similar happens, that is to say, you must denote a high degree of discipline at all times.

The "sacrifice" is also a point to consider in this "world". In fact, surely, many people have heard the phrase that "every sacrifice has its reward." In a way, this phrase is quite certain applied in this "world" and now it will be possible demonstrates with an example.

It is true that, year by year over a long period of years, you can see many people who have spent hours, days or even weeks to organize their holiday trips that will only last for one week. Likewise, surely, they will have spent an average of about c.u.1,000 (hereinafter the abbreviation c.u. = currency units will be used either to refer to Euros, Pounds, Dollars, Rubles or another Currency) per person, as it has been mentioned, just to enjoy it for a week.

Continuing with this example, the following questions could be: whether the people would be willing to "sacrifice" that vacation of one week and the time used in organizing the trip and they would be willing to use the c.u.1,000 for an investment in their future.

If the answer is affirmative, that's what it could be identified as "sacrifice" in this "world". Sometimes, it is necessary to "sacrifice" a holiday to try to get a better quality of life in the future.

If it is continued analyzing the example of holidays, between the results that could be obtained, we have shown the following:

Winner: first, people might have spent a marvelous and perfect vacation for a week and, therefore, they would think it was worth the c.u.1,000 spent as well as the time used to organize them; or conversely,

Loser: anyone can make the situation of which they encountered during their holidays in bad weather, transport strikes, and they were horrible holiday and, besides, they might think that it has not been worth the c.u. 1,000 used on the trip and the time taken to prepare their holidays.

In the "world of the Stock Exchange", the situation could have been similar, that is to say, they had invested c.u.1,000 in the stock market and these possible results could be obtained:

Winner: they had obtained spectacular profits that they will allow them to do, not just a one-week trip, including a trip of a month, in addition, they would be very satisfied with the time spent on preparing their investment; or conversely,

Loser: they had lost c.u. 1,000 invested, as well as they might think it would not worth the time spent to study investment.

Moreover, and probably one of the most important principles should be considered in a peculiar way the "LOVE", that is to say, keep always some degree of "Love" in everything we are doing. If "Love" is set in this "world", as well as any other "world" (family, labor or professional, personal, social ...), you could ensure that you WILL BE ALLWAYS THE WINNER.

That is, using "Love", where investments will go well, besides being WINNER, you will have a bonus that does not equate to money; and if the results are not as expected, surely you will continue being a WINNER, because it will allow you to learn from mistakes to improve and progress on future occasions.

Returning to the previous example about holidays and investment, if the results obtained as "Loser" we add the ingredient of "Love", we could transform it into a result as "Winner". Many people will wonder how I can transform a "Loser" result into a "Winner" result only adding "Love". Well, in many cases, you can hear the phrase that "Love many things are achieved," and in the "world of the Stock Exchange" can also be achieved.

If we include the "Love", the result considered "Loser" becomes "Winner". This "Loser" result have been one more experience where you can learn and you will be able to take into consideration to organize and improve the upcoming holidays -example, contracting a travel insurance covering bad weather, lost luggage, etc- or improve future investments -example, investing in different companies to diversify risk-. As you can see, applying the "Love", it has moved from the status of "Loser" to the status of "Winner".

If you are new to this "world" and you think you have these simple requirements, I am grateful to welcome you to the "world of the Stock Exchange" and you can consider that you have some of the conditions that you may route to the WINNER side.

7. ALL THAT GLITTERS IS NOT GOLD

Surely many people know or have read the article about the experiment that was conducted in 1973, where a monkey was given darts he threw on a financial newspaper. In this economic newspaper had included the companies listed on the Stock Exchange. Companies where the darts fell, they were taken as reference to compare the results of these companies with the results of the companies selected by "professionals" or "experts" in the Stock Exchange.

The result of this experiment was that the monkey obtained superior results compared with some of the "professionals or experts" of the Stock Exchange, that is to say, the result was better in the companies where monkey had selected throwing darts

In this experiment, conjectures have been exposed that it is not necessary to be a "professional" to invest in "Stock Exchange" and get good profitability and, therefore, the random is a part of the returns or profits.

But do not just keep in mind the concept that "any monkey" can invest in Stock Exchange and be "Winner". It is also true that the more knowledge on the functioning of the International Stock Exchange, also the chances of success are increased and risks associated with the investment are minimized.

Furthermore, this experiment is somewhat incomplete and may leave many gaps that must rethink:

- What would have happened if -in this experiment- the monkey had chosen the worst companies?

  No therefore we would have to say then, that the Stock Exchange is only for "professionals or experts" with high levels of expertise in economics, mathematics, statistics and other related sciences.

- Why did they choose "one monkey" and "several experts" on Stock Exchange in this experiment?

- What would have happened if they had chosen "several monkeys" and "one expert" on Stock Exchange?

- Was the experiment repeated by the same monkey?

  This monkey, specifically, did not return to repeat this experiment according to data that have been published.

With these questions, those just try to show that, in the experiment of the monkey", we cannot extrapolate and ensure that, whenever anyone throws some darts at random to make investments in companies, always yields to be obtained will be higher than the performance of the "professionals".

However, we know that this experiment was repeated for several years with other monkeys, and the results were that in the long term, in this case, the monkeys did not overcome the average returns of the "professionals".

With the example of this experiment, we try to convey that, in the lifetime, you can analyze a huge amount of information on this world of the Stock Exchange where there are many topics, systems, methods and so on. We must clarify that the "International Stock Exchange" is not an exact science. In "The Stock Exchange" 2 + 2 are not always 4, so when you make an investment, it is important to know the company or product where you are investing, the risk that you're going to take, and be aware that we are really who will decide where to invest.

8. SPEAKING ABOUT TRUTHS AND ALMOST TRUTHS

As previously, it has been demonstrated in the monkey experiment, it is necessary to evaluate and analyze the news that are received in its relative amount

In fact, the absolute truth by itself does not exist neither in the "world of the Stock Exchange" nor the "real world" where you live every day, that is, you could try to get with the sum of all relative truths to get the absolute truth.

Therefore, when you want to invest in the Stock Exchange, you should really know where you are investing, that is, you should know most of relative truths, because, if you do not know or are not sure where the savings will be invested, the best option is not to invest.

Therefore, when we want to invest in the International Stock Exchange, it is interesting to know the companies where we are going to invest. To be able to know the companies where we can invest in the International Stock Exchange, you can use two types of analysis:

- "Fundamental Analysis" of the company, that is, knowing the financial statements of companies, balance sheets, income statements, losses and profits, etc; and / or

- "Technical Analysis" of the company, that is, through graphics, convergences and divergences, volume, averages, Fibonacci, Japanese Candlestick, Bollinger bands, channels, media, supports, resistances, etc.

It is anticipated that the "system" which it will be explained in this book for investment in International Stock Exchange, is based and developed through what is known as Technical Analysis.

The "system" is adapted to each of the real international companies that will be exposed in real examples.

Furthermore, it is going to be demonstrated how this "system" has worked into reality through actual numerical data that are attached to each company that, in this book, has been studied.

Although as in this book indicates, it is important that YOU are the one that really you could evaluate if you are capable of this "system" fits and works in companies or products that YOU really know and want to invest.

In fact, before putting the "system" running with real money, it is always recommended that you should develop a simulation of the procedure of the "system" without real money. In case that there is any doubt regarding the procedure, you should not invest real money until this one or other tools are controlled properly.

9. THE MILLION DOLLAR QUESTION

A very common question among those who venture or want to invest in International Stock Exchange and is probably the question we try to answer more about this "world" is: Am I going to become rich on the Stock Exchange?

This question so common, it could be answered with another question that it will give you the solution, perhaps, are you going to become rich spending 8 or more hours a day in your workplace?

YOU have the answer to your question and it is very simple. As it has been indicated from the beginning of this book, it depends on only and exclusively of YOU.

If YOU know yourself well, you know exactly what you can be able to get, since the results will depend on factors such as effort, commitment, involvement, time used, knowledge, risk aversion -level afraid you have to lose-, that is to say, everything that you want to devote to this "world".

It is important to recall some of the pillars, aforementioned, to invest in the Stock Exchange as are: the Self-confidence, self-discipline, sacrifice and LOVE. Here are the main ingredients to complete the answers.

10. WHY ARE YOU WINNER OR LOSER? YOU DECIDE IT

In the lifetime, people have to take a position in one of the two extremes. And most important thing, in the majority of the cases, people can choose to be a Winner or Loser by themselves; in other cases, there are uncontrollable external factors and they are that make us to take position on one side or another.

Unfortunately, the economic crisis of 2007 that has been suffered worldwide, people have become more reluctant to trust the intermediaries or brokers in the moment to invest the savings. It has also been observed that many families have been ruined and they are in the street homeless due to the advice that once had recommended the intermediaries or brokers in which they were entrusted.

Although it is not possible to generalize, it is necessary to remember that the "intermediaries", "brokers" or "employees" are not really our friends. They have to get some benefits and some results. "Employees" have goals to achieve that they are marked by their companies in which they work. And partly to the fulfillment of these goals, the salaries of the "employees" are paid every week or every month.

"Employees" have neither to know about the Stock Exchange nor understand about their products. They only have to sell the products that managers have indicated to them to achieve goals.

On this premise, everyone should be worried where they invest the savings or, at least, know the product or company and, therefore, be aware that they are responsible for the decisions that they have considered to be carried out.

It is also interesting to consider other series of questions and dedicate a moment of reflection. It could be considered a basic question the following example, the question might be, why when people want to buy a car, they spend so much time and worry for knowing the minimum requirements of car that they want -car model, engine power, doors should have, big or small, color, etc- and also prices are compared in different locations and even the cars are tested before buying them?

Perhaps, when people buy a car, are they going directly to the first car shop where they find in their walk?, and do they usually tell the seller, "I want a car"?, and do they accept the first car that the seller offers them without doing any more questions?

This simple example shows us that, in general, people buy cars without the necessity of being "engineers", right?

Then, the next question could be why when people want to invest the savings -which have involved many hours of effort, time and work-, do not they spend a little more time and they try to know the product -name of the product, returns the product offers, the risk to take, etc- and people directly rely on what the "intermediaries" or "employees" tell them?

This is an interesting question that often many people should ask. Surely, some of the most common answers would be: either they do not have time or they are not "professionals or experts".

But if these responses are compared with the example of the car, the result obtained is more interesting, since, people have always had time to get information before buying the car and the features they wanted in spite of not being "engineers", on the other hand, the people to choose investments where they will deposit the saved money and could represent them a better quality of life for future, people have not had time or interest to know the product and directly, they have left the decision of investment to the "intermediary", "employee" or "broker".

Now with this simple example, anyone can know what position you want to be and if you really want to participate in the world of Stock Exchange, since, depending on one's decisions you choose, you will be in a position or another: Winner or Loser.

Therefore, it is crucial that you learn that in order that YOU WIN in the world of the Stock Exchange, OTHERS have to LOSE, that is to say, not everyone can be a WINNER in the Stock Exchange.

In this book, you only are going to find a "system" applied to examples about real cases that they have worked and that according to how you use it, the system will be able to place you in one side as WINNER or in other one as a LOSER, and nevertheless, YOU will be who really you decide which part to be.

11. PARADOX OF MATHEMATICS AND RISK CONTROL

In this section, we will see with one example more, something that in many occasions when you invest in the Stock Exchange is forgotten.

Well depending on what position the investor is, the investor may interpret the results of one way or another. Indeed, when you invest in the Stock Exchange, you have to keep in mind that sometimes the mathematics may appear somewhat different, according to the position in which the investor is.

We imagine two people who invest in one product:

- Alexander bought a "share" or "stock" for c.u. 80 and the share goes down its value in the Stock Exchange to 50%. Now, the value of the "share" of Alexander is c.u. 40 -Alexander in his mathematical reasoning has lost only 50%-.

- Peter buys the "share" now, and he only pays c.u. 40 -if Peter hopes that the share prices goes up to the price paid by Alexander, Peter will have earned 100%-.

When the share is increased up to the initial price of c.u. 80:

- Alexander will gain nothing -he bought for c.u. 80 and the price returns to c.u. 80-. In fact,

Alexander was losing 50%, and the share has needed to up the price 100%.

- Peter has won 100% -he bought c.u. 40 and the price is c.u. 80 now-.

It has become clear in the example, that although Alexander might have the feeling (mathematically) that he only had lost 50%, the reality is that the "share" had to raise 100% to recover his investment; on the other hand, Peter took the opportunity, and he got 100% of profitability.

With this example, we should also remember that before investing, it is very important to control the risk that implies each investment, and therefore it is necessary to limit the losses that you are willing to take depending on the level of risk each investor accepts.

One way to reduce exposure to risk is diversified investments, that is to say, the risk can be reduced by investing the money properly in different products.

12. WHAT DO WE NEED TO START?

As it has been mentioned along this book, the "system", that it is going to be applied, is based on Technical Analysis, that is to say, we are going to use graphs.

For that, firstly we would need -to work with this "system" in the Stock Exchange- to find a "intermediary" or "broker" where he could provide a "platform" -application or tool- to us that allows us to work graphically the price quote of the "share" or "stock" –companies- where we want to invest, and in addition on this platform, we could include the option of incorporating "moving average" inside the chart of the company or stock.

Currently, almost all platforms, that provide the intermediaries or brokers, work in a similar way. If the "intermediaries" or "broker" with which you work cannot provide the "platform" -including a graphic company and moving averages-, there is always the option to change the "intermediary" or "broker" or to look for online platform or website about economic news and the Stock Exchange.

The "system", that in this book is used, is essentially based on two basic parameters that are detailed below:

1. A graph, where there appears the price (or quote) of the "share" -company or product- where we want to invest.

2. The option where you are able to include in the chart a "moving average" to match the "share" -company or product-.

13. USE OF THE SYSTEM

In this section, it has been shown how you could use the "system", step by step, as well as how the system has been implemented in examples of different real companies randomly selected -similar to the experiment of monkeys-. In real cases, which will be used for example, have been used international companies that they are quoting in International Stock Exchange, although, they could be bonds, mutual funds, ETF, stock index, warrants, futures, currencies and so on.

When the "system" is applied in different companies in this book, it will be used a similar methodology in each of the companies. Therefore, if you are interested in reading the other two books **"GANADOR O PERDEDOR:** Todas las cosas que debes saber para invertir en todos los Mercados Internacionales Bursátiles… y algo más" and "**ПОБЕДИТЕЛЬ ИЛИ НЕУДАЧНИК:** все, что Вам нужно знать о том, как инвестировать в Международные Фондовые Биржи… и еще кое-что", without knowing the language it will be readily identifiable because the same system is used in other international companies and you can follow those great profits are obtained.

The "system", as it has been indicated previously, on the one hand consists of a graph where two lines are shown:

- -The staggered black line represents the price of the "stock" (company or product) throughout the time (days, weeks, months, etc).

- The grey line represents the moving average or "media móvil" (normally identified in the "platforms" as "MA" for English version or "MM" for Spanish version).

The "system" will consist basically of the following steps that are detailed below:

- Buy the "share" at the point where the staggered black line (price) crosses above the grey line (moving average).

- Keep the "share" while the staggered black line is above the grey line.

- Sell the "share" at the point where the staggered black line again crossed the grey line (this time the staggered black line is below the grey).

- Wait for returning to buy the "share" when the line crossing again, that is to say, the staggered black line above the grey line.

- Return to repeat the described steps. Easy, right?

Subsequently, following each graph, the next data are collected in tables:

- The name of the company according to study.

- The main points where lines prices and lines moving averages have crossed

- Buy transactions (black color) where it is indicated the exact date and buy price.

- Sales transactions (grey color) where it is indicated the exact date and sell price.

- Possible sales transactions -maximum price- (light grey color) with the exact date and sell price could have been achieved.

- Each table shows a different buy-sell transaction.

COMPANY	COMPANY'S NAME	
	Date	Price
(1)BUY:	MM-DD-YY	40,26
(1')SELL:	MM-DD-YY	43,74
(A)SELL (MAX.):	MM-DD-YY	46,47

Then it is shown in another table, both the profit (grey color) by using the "system", as well as the maximum profit (light grey color) that it could have been obtained while we had bought the "share".

PROFIT: (1')-(1)=43,74-40,26=3,48

PROFIT (MAX.): (A)-(1)=46,47-40,26=6,21

The following table shown indicates the percentage (grey color) is obtained by using the "system" as well as the maximum percentage (light grey color) we could have obtained while we had bought the "share".

PERCENTAGE: (1')-(1)=8,64 %

PERCENTAGE (MAX.): (A)-(1)=15,42 %

In the examples of real cases that we will see shortly, it has been used on the same company, charts daily prices and charts weekly prices, so it is possible to identify easily the differences in the results obtained by applying the same "system".

14. LET'S GO TO THE "ACTION"

As it has been explained in the previous section, in this section we proceed to the implementation of the "system" in the examples of real cases of randomly selected companies.

As we are going to be able to see, in each one of the graphs we have applied a different "moving average". This "moving average" is adapted to each company and depending on whether they are charts daily prices or charts weekly prices, we will obtain different results.

The graphs are displayed, the staggered black line is the evolution of the quoted price of the company over time; and the grey line is the moving average used.

The charts have been marked the key points for buying operations with a number (X), and the key points for selling operations with a number' (X'), likewise, it is marked with a capital letter (A) one of maximum prices that it could have been achieved in the operation.

In the tables, we have collected the results that they could have been obtained by applying the "system" both for pricing difference obtained and the percentage of each buying - selling transaction.

It is recalled that the actual data of the examples of these international companies are elaborated to date March 10, 2015, it being possible when the "system" was applied may be operations that could be found in processing scenario, that is to say, without the "system" indicates the sell price.

We start working with examples of real international companies:

In the company COCACOLA FEMSA (KOF) – USA

- Implementation of the "system" using a moving average of 450 sessions (grey line) in the *daily price chart* (staggered black line).

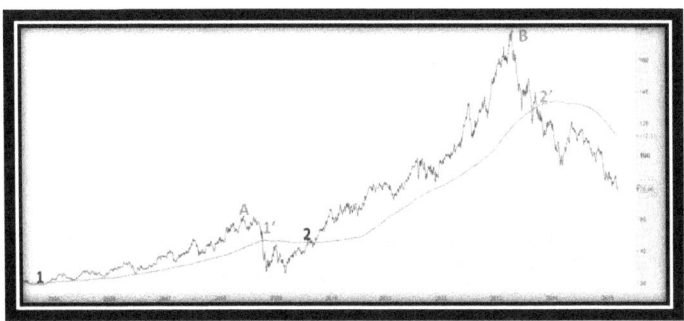

Operation Number 1:

COMPANY	COCACOLA (KOF)	
	Date	Price
(1)BUY:	11-11-04	21,19
(1')SELL:	10-03-08	47,17
(A)SELL (MAX.):	06-05-08	62,5

The profits obtained when the system uses, that is, the difference between the buy price and sell price are shown in grey.

Maximum profits that could be obtained using the system, that is, the difference between the buy price and maximum sell price are shown in light grey.

PROFIT: (1')-(1)=47,17-21,19=25,98

PROFIT (MAX.): (A)-(1)=62,5-21,19=41,31

Also in the above table, now the profits are expressed in percentage terms, and these are:

PERCENTAGE: (1')-(1)=122,61 %

PERCENTAGE (MAX.): (A)-(1)=194,95 %

Operation Number 2:

COMPANY	COCACOLA (KOF)	
	Date	Price
(2)BUY:	09-16-09	45,93
(2')SELL:	10-26-13	128,49
(B)SELL (MAX.):	04-24-13	166,58

The profits obtained using the system and the maximum profits that could be obtained are:

PROFIT: (2')-(2)=128,49-45,93=82,56

PROFIT (MAX.): (B)-(2)=166,58-45,93=120,65

In percentage terms, the profits are:

PERCENTAGE: (2')-(2)=179,75 %

PERCENTAGE (MAX.): (B)-(2)=262,68 %

- Implementation of the "system" using a moving average of 450 sessions (grey line) in *the weekly price chart* (staggered black line).

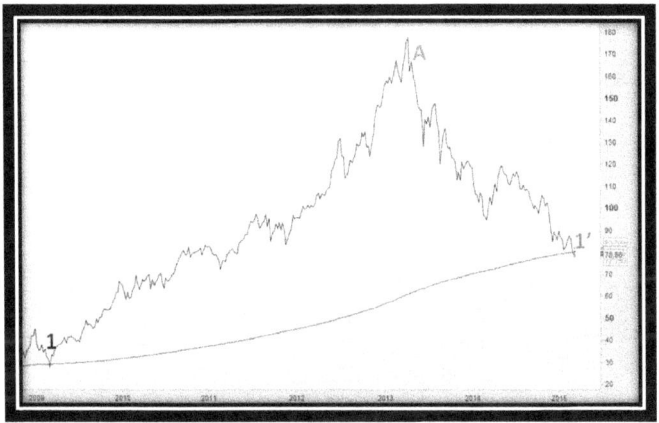

Operation Number 1:

COMPANY	COCACOLA (KOF)	
	Date	Price
(1)BUY:	03-09-09	29,11
(1')SELL:	03-02-15	80,09
(A)SELL (MAX.):	04-15-13	178,54

The profits obtained using the system and the maximum profits that could be obtained are:

PROFIT: (1')-(1)=80,09-29,11=50,98

PROFIT (MAX.): (A)-(1)=178,54-29,11=149,43

In percentage terms, the profits are:

PERCENTAGE: (1')-(1)= 175,13 %

PERCENTAGE (MAX.): (A)-(1)= 513,33 %

In the company MOBILE TELESYSTEMS (MTSS) - RUSSIA

- Implementation of the "system" using a moving average of 38 sessions (grey line) in the *daily price chart* (staggered black line).

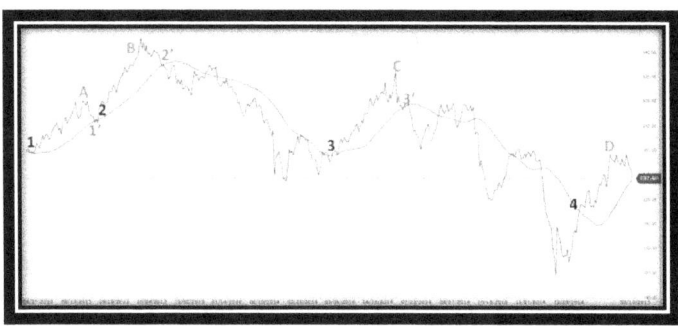

Operation Number 1:

COMPANY	MOBILE TELESYSTEM (MTSS)	
	Date	Price
(1)BUY:	06-27-13	259,24
(1')SELL:	08-30-13	283,47
(A)SELL (MAX.):	08-21-13	300,79

The profits obtained using the system and the maximum profits that could be obtained are:

PROFIT: (1')-(1)=283,47-259,24=24,23

PROFIT (MAX.): (A)-(1)=300,79-259,24=41,55

In percentage terms, the profits are:

PERCENTAGE: (1')-(1)=9,35 %

PERCENTAGE (MAX.): (A)-(1)=16,03 %

Operation Number 2:

COMPANY	MOBILE TELESYSTEM (MTSS)	
	Date	Price
(2)BUY:	09-04-13	284,81
(2')SELL:	11-06-13	328,9
(B)SELL (MAX.):	10-16-13	351.5

The profits obtained using the system and the maximum profits that could be obtained are:

PROFIT: (2')-(2)=328,9-284,81=44,09

PROFIT (MAX.): (B)-(2)= 351,5-284,81=66,69

In percentage terms, the profits are:

PERCENTAGE: (2')-(2)=15,48 %

PERCENTAGE (MAX.): (B)-(2)=23,42 %

Operation Number 3:

COMPANY	MOBILE TELESYSTEM (MTSS)	
	Date	Price
(3)BUY:	04-29-14	256,2
(3')SELL:	07-09-14	294,25
(C)SELL (MAX.):	07-03-14	324

The profits obtained using the system and the maximum profits that could be obtained are:

PROFIT: (3')-(3)=294,25-256,2=38,05

PROFIT (MAX.): (C)-(3)=324-256,2=67,8

In percentage terms, the profits are:

PERCENTAGE: (3')-(3)=14,85 %

PERCENTAGE (MAX.): (C)-(3)=26,46 %

Operation Number 4:

COMPANY	MOBILE TELESYSTEM (MTSS)	
	Date	Price
(4)BUY:	04-14-15	211,21
(4')SELL:	IN PROGRESS	
(D)SELL (MAX.):	02-13-15	257,35

The profits obtained using the system and the maximum profits that could be obtained are:

PROFIT: (4')-(4)=IN PROGRESS

PROFIT (MAX.): (D)-(4)=257,35-211,21=46,14

In percentage terms, the profits are:

PERCENTAGE: (4')-(4)=IN PROGRESS

PERCENTAGE (MAX.): (D)-(4)=21,85 %

- Implementation of the "system" using a moving average of 60 sessions (grey line) in *the weekly price chart* (staggered black line).

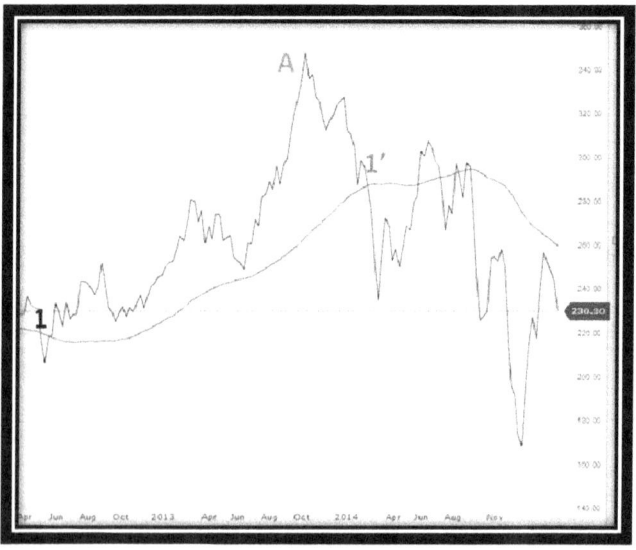

Operation Number 1:

COMPANY	MOBILE TELESYSTEM (MTSS)	
	Date	Price
(1)BUY:	05-20-12	218,99
(1')SELL:	02-16-14	287,81
(A)SELL (MAX.):	10-13-13	348,86

The profits obtained using the system and the maximum profits that could be obtained are:

PROFIT: (1')-(1)=287,81-218,99=68,82

PROFIT (MAX.): (A)-(1)=348,86-218,99=129,87

In percentage terms, the profits are:

PERCENTAGE: (1')-(1)=31,43 %

PERCENTAGE (MAX.): (A)-(1)=59,30 %

In the company INDITEX (ITX) - SPAIN

- Implementation of the "system" using a moving average of 360 sessions (grey line) in the *daily price chart* (staggered black line).

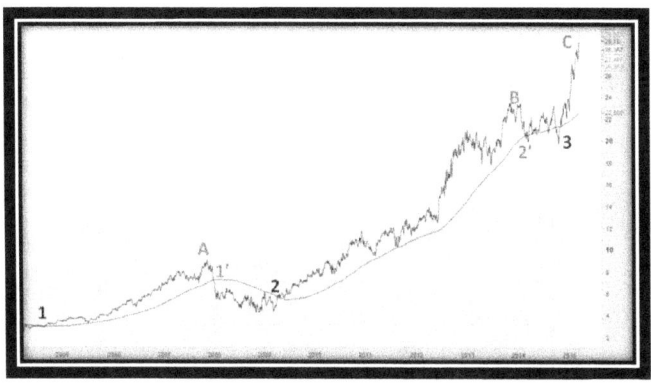

Operation Number 1:

COMPANY	INDITEX (ITX)	
	Date	Price
(1)BUY:	08-24-04	2,98
(1')SELL:	12-21-07	7,26
(A)SELL (MAX.):	11-07-07	9,13

The profits obtained using the system and the maximum profits that could be obtained are:

PROFIT: (1')-(1)=7,26-2,98=4,28

PROFIT (MAX.): (A)-(1)=9,13-2,98=6,15

In percentage terms, the profits are:

PERCENTAGE: (1')-(1)=143,62 %

PERCENTAGE (MAX.): (A)-(1)=206,38 %

Operation Number 2:

COMPANY	INDITEX (ITX)	
	Date	Price
(2)BUY:	04-29-09	5,59
(2')SELL:	02-27-14	20,48
(B)SELL (MAX.):	10-31-13	23,51

The profits obtained using the system and the maximum profits that could be obtained are:

PROFIT: (2')-(2)=20,48-5,59=14,89

PROFIT (MAX.): (B)-(2)=23,51-5,59=17,92

In percentage terms, the profits are:

PERCENTAGE: (2')-(2)=266,37 %

PERCENTAGE (MAX.): (B)-(2)=320,57 %

Operation Number 3:

COMPANY	INDITEX (ITX)	
	Date	Price
(3)BUY:	10-27-14	21,32
(3')SELL:	IN PROGRESS	
(C)SELL (MAX.):	03-18-15	29,15

The profits obtained using the system and the maximum profits that could be obtained are:

PROFIT: (3')-(3)=IN PROGRESS

PROFIT (MAX.): (C)-(3)=29,15-21,32=7,83

In percentage terms, the profits are:

PERCENTAGE: (3')-(3)=IN PROGRESS

PERCENTAGE (MAX.): (C)-(3)=36,73 %

- Implementation of the "system" using a moving average of 390 sessions (grey line) in *the weekly price chart* (staggered black line).

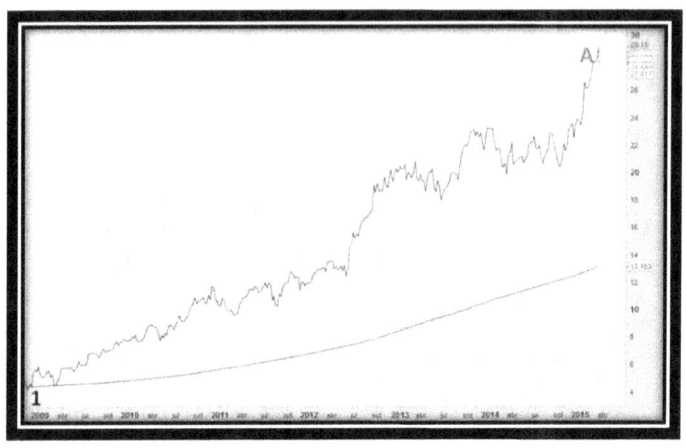

Operation Number 1:

COMPANY	INDITEX (ITX)	
	Date	Price
(1)BUY:	11-24-08	4,46
(1')SELL:	IN PROGRESS	
(A)SELL (MAX.):	03-18-15	29,15

The profits obtained using the system and the maximum profits that could be obtained are:

PROFIT: (1')-(1)=IN PROGRESS

PROFIT (MAX.): (A)-(1)=29,15-4,46=24,69

In percentage terms, the profits are:

PERCENTAGE: (1')-(1)=IN PROGRESS

PERCENTAGE MAX.: (A)-(1)= 553,59 %

15. USING THE "SYSTEM" IN AMERICAN AND EUROPEAN COMPANIES

Once we know the use of the "system" in the examples of international companies shown in the previous section, we will continue using the "system" with examples of American and European companies.

The methodology that we are going to use in the examples of American and European companies are the same as it was used in the examples of international companies that have been explained above.

It will be adapted the "moving average" to the next companies and they will get these results:

In the company APPLE INC (AAPL) - USA

- Implementation of the "system" using a moving average of 250 sessions (grey line) in the *daily price chart* (staggered black line).

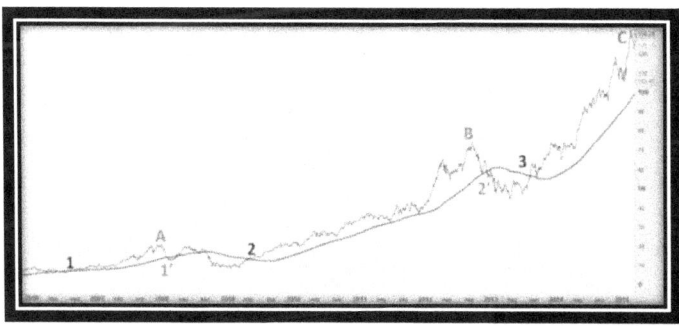

Operation Number 1:

COMPANY	APPLE INC (AAPL)	
	Date	Price
(1)BUY:	07-26-06	6,33
(1')SELL:	01-24-08	13,64
(A)SELL (MAX.):	12-27-07	20,29

The profits obtained using the system and the maximum profits that could be obtained are:

PROFIT: (1')-(1)=13,64-6,33=7,31.

PROFIT (MAX.): (A)-(1)=20,29-6,33=13,96

In percentage terms, the profits are:

PERCENTAGE: (1')-(1)=115,48%

PERCENTAGE (MAX.):(A)-(1)=220,54%

Operation Number 2:

COMPANY	APPLE INC (AAPL)	
	Date	Price
(2)BUY:	05-26-09	12,61
(2')SELL:	12-05-12	58,73
(B)SELL (MAX.):	09-19-12	73,95

The profits obtained using the system and the maximum profits that could be obtained are:

PROFIT: (2')-(2)=58,73-12,61=46,12

PROFIT (MAX.):(B)-(2)=73,95-12,61=61,34

In percentage terms, the profits are:

PERCENTAGE: (2')-(2)=365,74%

PERCENTAGE (MAX.):(B)-(2)=486,44%

Operation Number 3:

COMPANY	APPLE INC (AAPL)	
	Date	Price
(3)BUY:	08-08-13	56,64
(3')SELL:	IN PROGRESS	
(C)SELL (MAX.):	02-24-15	132,17

The profits obtained using the system and the maximum profits that could be obtained are:

PROFIT:(3')-(3)=IN PROGRESS

PROFIT (MAX.):(C)-(3)=132,17-56,64=75,53

In percentage terms, the profits are:

- Implementation of the "system" using a moving average of 250 sessions (grey line) in *the weekly price chart* (staggered black line).

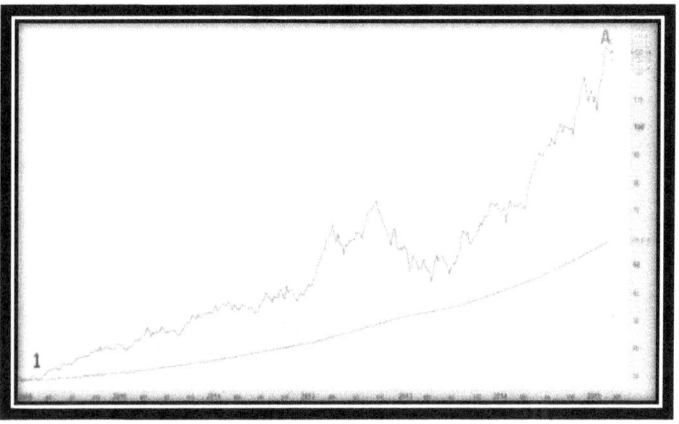

Operation Number 1:

COMPANY	APPLE INC (AAPL)	
	Date	Price
(1)BUY:	03-02-09	8,89
(1')SELL:	IN PROGRESS	
(A)SELL (MAX.):	02-16-15	129,5

The profits obtained using the system and the maximum profits that could be obtained are:

PROFIT:(1')-(1)=IN PROGRESS

PROFIT (MAX.):(A)-(1)=129,5-8,89=120,61

In percentage terms, the profits are:

PERCENTAGE:(1')-(1)=IN PROGRESS

PERCENTAGE (MAX.):(A)-(1)=1356,69%

In the company VOLKSWAGEN AG ST (VOW) – EUROPE (GERMANY)

- Implementation of the "system" using a moving average of 450 sessions (grey line) in the *daily price chart* (staggered black line).

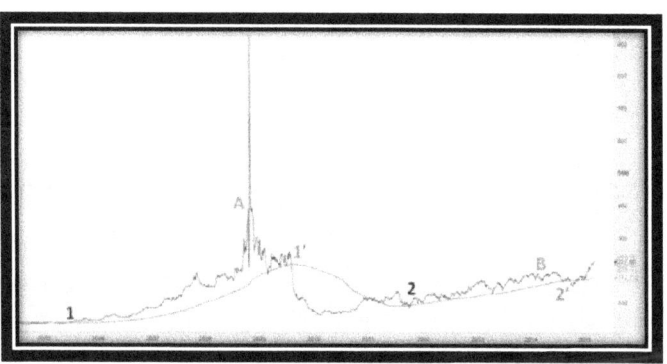

Operation Number 1:

COMPANY	VOLKSWAGEN AGST O.N. (VOW)	
	Date	Price
(1)BUY:	06-15-05	34,92
(1')SELL:	02-27-09	193,81
(A)SELL (MAX.):	10-16-08	390

The profits obtained using the system and the maximum profits that could be obtained are:

PROFIT:(1')-(1)=193,81-34,92=158,89

PROFIT (MAX.):(A)-(1)=390-34,92=355.08

In percentage terms, the profits are:

PERCENTAGE:(1')-(1)=115,48%

PERCENTAGE (MAX.):(A)-(1)=220,54%

Operation Number 2:

COMPANY	VOLKSWAGEN AGST O.N. (VOW)	
	Date	Price
(2)BUY:	10-11-11	91,16
(2')SELL:	07-30-14	167,98
(B)SELL (MAX.):	05-03-14	193.00

The profits obtained using the system and the maximum profits that could be obtained are:

PROFIT:(2')-(2)=167,98-91,16=76,82

PROFIT (MAX.):(B)-(2)=193-91,16=101,84

In percentage terms, the profits are:

PERCENTAGE:(2')-(2)=84,27%

PERCENTAGE (MAX.):(B)-(2)=111,72%

- Implementation of the "system" using a moving average of 450 sessions (grey line) in _the weekly price chart_ (staggered black line).

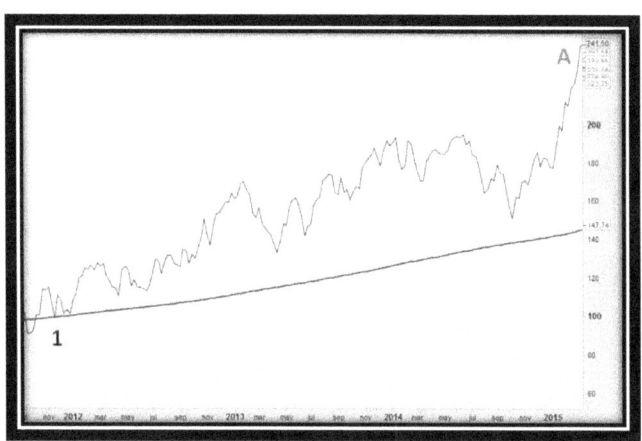

Operation Number 1:

COMPANY	VOLKSWAGEN AGST O.N. (VOW)	
	Date	Price
(1)BUY:	11-21-11	99,48
(1')SELL:	IN PROGRESS	
(A)SELL (MAX.):	03-02-15	227,9

The profits obtained using the system and the maximum profits that could be obtained are:

PROFIT:(1')-(1)=IN PROGRESS

PROFIT (MAX.):(A)-(1)=227,9-99,48=128,42

In percentage terms, the profits are:

PERCENTAGE:(1')-(1)=IN PROGRESS

PERCENTAGE (MAX.):(A)-(1)=129,09%

In the company LLOYDS GRP. (LLOY) – EUROPE (UNITED KINGDOM)

- Implementation of the "system" using a moving average of 155 sessions (grey line) in the *daily price chart* (staggered black line).

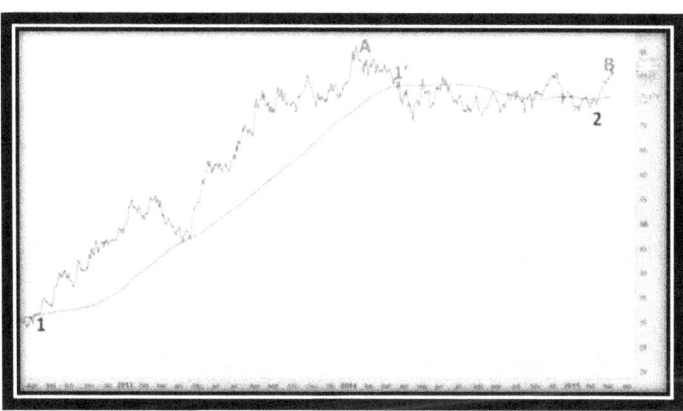

Operation Number 1:

COMPANY	LLOYDS GRP. (LLOY)	
	Date	Price
(1)BUY:	08-10-12	31,29
(1')SELL:	03-20-14	78,09
(A)SELL (MAX.):	01-15-14	86,3

The profits obtained using the system and the maximum profits that could be obtained are:

PROFIT:(1')-(1)=78,09-31,29=46,8

PROFIT (MAX.):(A)-(1)=86,3-31,29=55,01.

In percentage terms, the profits are:

PERCENTAGE:(1')-(1)=149,57%

PERCENTAGE (MAX.):(A)-(1)=175,81%

Operation Number 2:

COMPANY	LLOYDS GRP. (LLOY)	
	Date	Price
(2)BUY:	02-13-15	75,43
(2')SELL:	IN PROGRESS	
(B)SELL (MAX.):	03-06-15	81,43

The profits obtained using the system and the maximum profits that could be obtained are:

PROFIT:(2')-(2)=IN PROGRESS

PROFIT (MAX.):(B)-(2)=81,43-75,43=6

In percentage terms, the profits are:

PERCENTAGE:(2')-(2)=IN PROGRESS

PERCENTAGE (MAX.):(B)-(2)=7,95%

- Implementation of the "system" using a moving average of 155 sessions (grey line) in *the weekly price chart* (staggered black line).

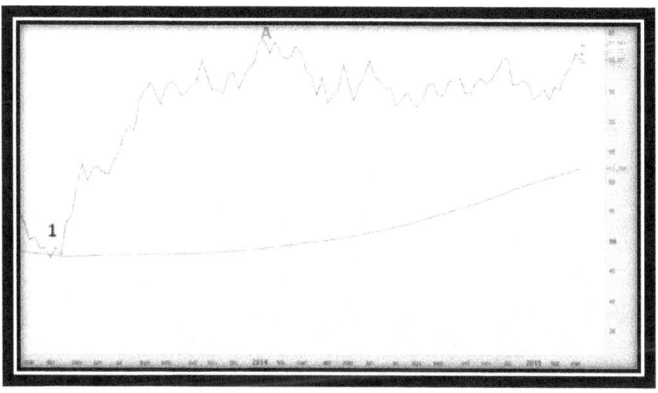

Operation Number 1:

COMPANY	LLOYDS GRP. (LLOY)	
	Date	Price
(1)BUY:	04-01-13	47,51
(1')SELL:	IN PROGRESS	
(A)SELL (MAX.):	01-13-14	83,52

The profits obtained using the system and the maximum profits that could be obtained are:

PROFIT:(1')-(1)=IN PROGRESS

PROFIT (MAX.):(A)-(1)=83,52-47,51=36,01

In percentage terms, the profits are:

PERCENTAGE:(1')-(1)=IN PROGRESS

PERCENTAGE (MAX.):(A)-(1)=75,79%

16. LET YOUR MONEY WORK FOR YOU

As summary, you have seen in this book by the examples of real companies that have been appeared and analyzed previously, that with the knowledge of this simple "system" and being implemented in an appropriate way in the examples shown, they might have been able to obtain great real profits.

Now that you know this tool and how the "system" is used, YOU should decide if you are ready to use or continue studying more about the world of the Stock Exchange.

Likewise, if you are interested in knowing the excellent profits that have been obtained using the same "system" in other examples of Spanish companies, South American companies and Russian companies, it is interesting that you see examples of actual cases that have been used in other two books **"GANADOR O PERDEDOR:** Todas las cosas que debes saber para invertir en todos los Mercados Internacionales Bursátiles… y algo más" and "**ПОБЕДИТЕЛЬ ИЛИ НЕУДАЧНИК:** все, что Вам нужно знать о том, как инвестировать в Международные Фондовые Биржи… и еще кое-что".

I wish that it was interesting and helpful the knowledge acquired in this book and they may have increased your knowledge about other investment alternatives or to improve your future investments.

And that's all, as you have verified, the system works and is very simple to implement.

From here everything is in your hands ... YOU choose if you keep letting advice from others and they manage your money for you, or YOU are who take your own decisions.

17. ACKNOWLEDGMENTS

I'll start with a question about the title of this book: Winner or Loser?

I feel WINNER, not only for the fact of taking part in the world of the Stock Exchange, plus I feel WINNER to have marvelous parents, relative, friends, colleagues and above all also, I feel WINNER and happy by not sitting watching life pass from the sidelines but to be and take part actively participating in life. So I hope I have helped with the publication of this book and the other two books **"GANADOR O PERDEDOR:** Todas las cosas que debes saber para invertir en todos los Mercados Internacionales Bursátiles… y algo más" and **"ПОБЕДИТЕЛЬ ИЛИ НЕУДАЧНИК:** все, что Вам нужно знать о том, как инвестировать в Международные Фондовые Биржи… и еще кое-что", that many more people are WINNERS and they understand a little better how the world of the Stock Exchange works, since not only money brings happiness. SHARE AND LIVE THE LIFE. But as I have repeated in several occasions, the last decision is in YOU.

My special thanks to all people at all times, who have helped me, supported, accompanied, collaborated and participated in this project.

Thanks to you, it has been possible to make a dream come true. That dream that one day I had in mind and it has been realized and capture through this book and the other two books **"GANADOR O PERDEDOR:** Todas las cosas que debes saber para invertir en todos los Mercados Internacionales Bursátiles... y algo más" and **"ПОБЕДИТЕЛЬ ИЛИ НЕУДАЧНИК:** все, что Вам нужно знать о том, как инвестировать в Международные Фондовые Биржи... и еще кое-что".

Undoubtedly, it is welcome, especially the work done, the effort and time spent, people who collaborated on the book "ПОБЕДИТЕЛЬ ИЛИ НЕУДАЧНИК: все, что Вам нужно знать о том, как инвестировать в Международные Фондовые Биржи... и еще кое-что".

And also thanks a lot to all those who have been attentive to the evolution of this project.

And of course, thank you very much **YOU** for reading this book and timeshare.

Remember: Life is not just Stock Exchange and to have a perfect life is fundamental to find the balance among health, love and wealth.

However, I am forever grateful and it will be nice the possibility to actively participate in other projects, conferences, seminars or events where we could transmit this or other systems of investment or savings and where there could be

offered the dissemination and knowledge of "financial education", as there also develop and share new ideas and are given the opportunity to let your money work for you.

We may be in continuous contact by Facebook:

http://www.facebook.com/rufino.villen

Once more THANK YOU VERY MUCH.